# Warriors of [illegible]ncient World: Legends of Courage and Honor

Shah Rukh

Published by Shah Rukh, 2024.

WARRIORS OF THE ANCIENT WORLD: LEGENDS OF COURAGE AND HONOR

**First edition. November 18, 2024.**



ISBN: 979-8230883142

Written by Shah Rukh.

# Table of Contents

# Prologue

For thousands of years, brave men and women have taken up arms to protect their people, fight for justice, and shape the course of history. These warriors weren't just soldiers—they were heroes who carried the weight of their societies on their shoulders. With courage in their hearts and unmatched skill in their hands, they stepped onto battlefields not only to conquer but also to defend what they held dear.

This book is a journey through time, exploring the lives of the ancient world's most legendary warriors. From the disciplined Spartans of Greece to the cunning Samurai of Japan, from Viking raiders crossing icy seas to Native American warriors protecting their lands, each chapter tells the story of individuals who lived by codes of honor and courage.

But warriors weren't only about fighting. They had beliefs, traditions, and values that guided them. They trained for years, honing their skills to perfection. They carried weapons that were as unique as their cultures, and their tales of bravery became the stuff of legend. Some fought for freedom, others for their kings, and many simply for survival.

As we explore the stories of these warriors, you'll discover how their battles, strategies, and unwavering bravery left lasting marks on history. You'll meet leaders who inspired their troops, warriors who became symbols of resilience, and even those who found honor in unexpected places.

Get ready to step into a world of ancient armies, secret battle tactics, and incredible feats of courage. These are the stories of the warriors who lived and fought with honor, shaping the ancient world as we know it.

# Chapter 1: The Rise of the Spartan Soldier

Long ago, in ancient Greece, there was a city called Sparta, famous for its fearless warriors. These soldiers weren't just any ordinary fighters—they were trained from a very young age to be some of the toughest and bravest people in history. But how did they become so legendary? Let's dive into their story.

In Sparta, being a soldier wasn't just a job; it was the most important thing in life. Spartans believed that their city needed strong protectors, and everyone worked together to make sure their warriors were the best. Boys in Sparta didn't grow up like kids in other places. Instead of spending most of their time playing games or learning art and music, they started preparing to be soldiers when they were very young. At just seven years old, boys were sent to a special training program called the *agoge*. It was like a school, but instead of regular classes, the boys learned how to fight, survive, and stay tough no matter what challenges came their way.

The *agoge* wasn't easy. The boys had to leave their families and live in groups called barracks with other boys their age. They learned how to use weapons like spears and shields, but they also learned how to endure hardships. For example, they were given only a small amount of food to eat, so they sometimes had to sneak or "steal" food to survive. However, if they got caught stealing, they were punished—not for stealing itself but for being careless enough to get caught! This taught them how to be clever and resourceful, skills that would help them on the battlefield.

Training wasn't just about fighting. The boys also learned how to obey orders without question. Spartans believed that soldiers who worked together like a well-oiled machine could defeat any enemy, no matter how strong. They practiced marching in perfect lines, holding their shields in a way that created a solid wall of protection called a *phalanx*. This teamwork was one of the things that made Spartan armies so powerful.

As they grew older, the boys faced tougher and tougher challenges. By the time they were in their teens, they were already skilled warriors. They learned how to fight not just with weapons but also with their bare hands. They also had to endure harsh conditions, like sleeping outside in the cold without blankets, to make their bodies strong and resistant to pain. Every part of their training was designed to prepare them for the hardships of war.

Once a Spartan boy turned 20, he officially became a soldier and joined the Spartan army. But even then, his training didn't stop. Spartan men continued to train every day, staying in peak condition so they were always ready to fight. They lived with their fellow soldiers in the barracks until they were 30 years old. This helped them stay focused on their duties and form strong bonds with their comrades.

Spartan soldiers were known for their courage and discipline. One of their most famous beliefs was that they should never retreat or surrender in battle. They were taught that it was better to die fighting for Sparta than to run away. This made them incredibly brave and respected by their enemies. A Spartan soldier's shield was especially important. It wasn't just for protecting himself but also for protecting the soldier next to him in the *phalanx*. Losing your shield in battle was considered a terrible disgrace because it meant you had let your comrades down.

Women in Sparta also played an important role in the rise of the Spartan soldier. While they didn't fight in battles, they were strong and independent. Spartan women managed the households and supported their husbands and sons. They encouraged their sons to be brave and reminded them of their duty to Sparta. One famous Spartan saying was, "Come back with your shield or on it," meaning that a soldier should return home victorious or die honorably in battle.

The Spartan way of life wasn't easy, but it created some of the most formidable warriors the world has ever known. Spartans fought in many famous battles, such as the Battle of Thermopylae, where 300 Spartan soldiers, led by King Leonidas, held off a massive Persian army for several days. Even though the Spartans were outnumbered, their courage and skill became legendary.

The rise of the Spartan soldier wasn't just about strength and fighting skills; it was also about dedication, discipline, and teamwork. Every Spartan grew up knowing that they were part of something greater than themselves—a community that valued bravery, honor, and sacrifice. This dedication made the Spartan soldiers stand out in history as some of the greatest warriors of all time.

# Chapter 2: Samurai of Japan: Masters of the Sword

Long ago, in the beautiful and mountainous islands of Japan, there lived a group of highly skilled warriors known as the samurai. These warriors weren't just fighters; they were experts in many arts, loyal to their lords, and guided by a strict code of honor. The samurai were masters of the sword, and their story is one of courage, discipline, and tradition that still fascinates people today.

The word "samurai" means "to serve," and that's exactly what these warriors did. Samurai dedicated their lives to serving their lords, called *daimyos*, who were powerful landowners in feudal Japan. In return, the lords provided the samurai with land, food, and protection for their families. Samurai didn't fight for personal glory; they fought to protect their lords and the lands they governed. This loyalty was one of the most important parts of being a samurai.

A samurai's training began in childhood. Boys born into samurai families started learning the ways of the warrior from a very young age. They were trained in the use of weapons like the bow and arrow, the spear, and most famously, the sword. But their training wasn't limited to combat. Samurai also studied reading, writing, and calligraphy to ensure they were as wise and disciplined in their minds as they were strong in their bodies. Many samurai were also trained in poetry and the arts, believing that true strength came from balancing skill in battle with wisdom and creativity.

At the heart of the samurai's training was their mastery of the sword, or *katana*. The *katana* was more than just a weapon; it was a symbol of the samurai's honor and spirit. Samurai treated their swords with the greatest respect, often giving them names and caring for them as if they were living beings. A samurai's sword was said to be an extension of their soul, and losing it was considered a terrible shame. These swords were carefully crafted by skilled artisans, and their sharpness, balance, and beauty made them some of the finest weapons in history.

The samurai didn't just learn how to use their swords—they trained tirelessly to become masters of every move. They practiced *kenjutsu*, the art of sword fighting, for hours every day. Their techniques weren't just about strength but also about precision, speed, and focus. Samurai believed in achieving a state of *zanshin*, or complete awareness, where they could react instantly and perfectly to any threat. This intense training made them nearly unbeatable in battle.

The samurai followed a strict code of honor called *bushido*, which means "the way of the warrior." This code emphasized values like loyalty, courage, respect, and self-discipline. Samurai were expected to be fearless in battle and to face danger with calm determination. If a samurai failed in their duty or dishonored their lord, they might choose to commit *seppuku*, a form of ritual suicide, to restore their honor. This shows how seriously they took their commitment to *bushido*.

But the life of a samurai wasn't all about fighting. They also had responsibilities in times of peace. Many samurai served as advisors to their lords, managed land, and helped settle disputes among the people. They were expected to set an example of discipline and integrity for others to follow. In this way, samurai were not only warriors but also leaders in their communities.

Samurai armor was another fascinating part of their life. Unlike the heavy suits of armor worn by knights in Europe, samurai armor was designed to be lightweight and flexible. It was made from small plates of metal bound together with leather or silk cords, which allowed the samurai to move quickly and fight skillfully. The armor was also beautifully decorated, often featuring symbols that represented the samurai's family or beliefs. Their helmets, called *kabuto*, were especially elaborate, sometimes adorned with horns, crests, or fierce designs to intimidate their enemies.

During Japan's feudal era, the samurai fought in many famous battles and wars. One of the most important periods in samurai history was the Sengoku period, also known as the Warring States period, when rival lords fought for control of the country. Samurai played a key role in these battles, leading armies and proving their skill and bravery on the battlefield. Legendary samurai like Miyamoto Musashi and Oda Nobunaga became famous for their strategies and strength, inspiring countless stories and legends.

Over time, the role of the samurai began to change. In the 1600s, under the Tokugawa shogunate, Japan entered a long period of peace, and samurai had fewer battles to fight. Many samurai took on new roles as government officials, teachers, or scholars, but they continued to live by the principles of *bushido*. The era of the samurai as warriors officially ended in the late 1800s, when Japan modernized its military and abolished the samurai class. However, their legacy lives on in Japanese culture.

Today, the samurai are remembered as symbols of bravery, discipline, and honor. Their swords, armor, and stories are displayed in museums, and their code of *bushido* continues to inspire people around the world. Martial arts like kendo, which is based on samurai sword fighting, are still practiced today, keeping the spirit of the samurai alive.

The samurai were more than just warriors; they were a unique blend of strength, wisdom, and loyalty. Their dedication to their craft, their lords, and their values made them some of the most respected and fascinating figures in history. They remind us that being a warrior isn't just about fighting—it's about living with honor, discipline, and purpose.

# Chapter 3: Gladiators in the Roman Arena

In ancient Rome, thousands of people would gather in huge arenas to watch thrilling battles between warriors called gladiators. These men, and sometimes even women, became symbols of bravery, strength, and the fierce entertainment of the Roman Empire. Their lives were filled with intense training, deadly combat, and moments of fame, but also great danger. Gladiators weren't just fighters; they were performers, warriors, and often prisoners who captivated audiences with their skill and courage.

The word "gladiator" comes from the Latin word *gladius*, which means "sword." This makes sense because most gladiators were armed with swords, although many used other weapons, too. Gladiators came from all walks of life. Some were prisoners of war from lands conquered by the Romans, while others were criminals or slaves who were forced into the arena. Surprisingly, some people became gladiators by choice. These individuals, called *auctorati*, often did so because they needed money or sought fame and glory. While they faced the same risks as other gladiators, they often had more freedom and better treatment.

Before stepping into the arena, gladiators went through intense training in special schools called *ludi*. These schools were run by trainers known as *lanistae*, who were often former gladiators themselves. The *lanistae* were experts in teaching fighting techniques, building strength, and preparing gladiators for the brutal challenges ahead. Each gladiator was trained in a specific style of combat, depending on their physical abilities and the weapons they used. Some specialized in heavy armor and large shields, while others focused on speed and agility, wearing little protection but relying on quick movements to avoid attacks.

One of the most famous types of gladiators was the *murmillo*. These warriors fought with a sword and a large rectangular shield and wore a helmet with a fish-shaped crest. Another type, the *retiarius*, fought with a trident and a net, trying to trap and stab their opponents. The *secutor* was often paired against the *retiarius* and wore a smooth helmet designed to deflect the trident. There were also *thracians*, who carried small round shields and curved swords, and *samnites*, who were heavily armored and used large shields and swords. Each type of gladiator had its strengths and weaknesses, making matches unpredictable and exciting for the audience.

Gladiatorial games were held in massive arenas, the most famous of which was the Colosseum in Rome. This enormous amphitheater could hold tens of thousands of spectators, all eager to watch the battles. The games weren't just about fighting; they were elaborate spectacles designed to entertain and impress the public. Events often began with parades, music, and performances. Gladiators would march into the arena, saluting the emperor or whoever was hosting the games, and shouting, "We who are about to die salute you!"

The fights themselves were dramatic and dangerous. Gladiators didn't always fight to the death, though that did happen in some cases. The outcome of a match often depended on the crowd's reaction. If a gladiator was defeated but had fought bravely, the audience or the emperor might spare their life. This decision was often signaled by a thumbs-up or thumbs-down gesture, though historians debate exactly how these gestures were used. A victorious gladiator could earn prizes, money, and even their freedom if they performed well over time.

Gladiators' lives were filled with risks, but they were also treated like celebrities in some ways. Victorious gladiators became famous, with fans cheering for them and even carving their names and images into walls as graffiti. Some wealthy Romans admired them so much that they invited them to parties or used their images in art and decorations. Despite their fame, gladiators lived under strict rules and were often treated as property by their *lanistae*. Their freedom was limited, and they could be punished severely for disobedience.

Women also participated in gladiatorial games, though their involvement was rare and often considered a novelty. Female gladiators, called *gladiatrices*, usually fought in smaller arenas and were seen as unusual and exotic. While they didn't achieve the same level of fame as their male counterparts, their participation added another layer of excitement to the games.

Gladiatorial games weren't just about individual battles. Sometimes, the events included large-scale mock battles called *naumachiae*, where entire groups of fighters would recreate famous military engagements. In some cases, the arena floor was even flooded to stage naval battles with boats and warriors. Other times, wild animals like lions, tigers, and elephants were brought into the arena to fight gladiators or other animals. These events, called *venationes*, were dangerous and thrilling, showcasing the Romans' ability to capture and control exotic creatures from faraway lands.

The games weren't only about entertainment; they also had a political purpose. Emperors and wealthy citizens used gladiatorial games to gain favor with the public. By hosting these extravagant events, they showed off their wealth and power while keeping the population entertained and distracted from political issues. For the spectators, the games were a way to experience the excitement of combat without any personal danger. They cheered for their favorite fighters and reveled in the drama of life-and-death battles.

Over time, the popularity of gladiatorial games began to decline. As the Roman Empire faced economic challenges and shifting cultural values, fewer resources were devoted to the games. By the 5th century CE, gladiatorial combat had mostly disappeared. The rise of Christianity also played a role, as many Christians opposed the violence and cruelty of the games.

Today, gladiators are remembered as symbols of ancient Rome's fascination with bravery, skill, and spectacle. Their story is both inspiring and tragic, showing the extremes of human strength and the harsh realities of life in the arena. The Colosseum and other ancient amphitheaters still stand as reminders of their incredible legacy, drawing visitors from around the world who are eager to learn about these legendary warriors. Although the days of gladiatorial combat are long gone, the courage and resilience of the gladiators continue to capture our imagination.

# Chapter 4: The Brave Archers of Mongolia

In the vast grasslands and rugged mountains of Mongolia, a group of fearless warriors mastered one of the most powerful and effective weapons in history: the bow and arrow. These were the brave Mongolian archers, whose skill and precision helped create one of the largest empires the world has ever known. Their story is one of unmatched expertise, innovative techniques, and incredible courage that changed the course of history.

The Mongolian archers were part of the mighty armies of Genghis Khan, the founder of the Mongol Empire in the 13th century. Genghis Khan understood that speed, mobility, and strategy were the keys to victory, and archers played a central role in his military tactics. Unlike other warriors who relied heavily on swords or spears, Mongolian archers were famous for fighting on horseback, shooting their arrows with deadly accuracy even while galloping at full speed. This ability gave them a huge advantage over their enemies.

To become such skilled archers, the Mongols started training at a very young age. Children in Mongolia grew up riding horses and practicing archery as part of their daily lives. By the time they were old enough to join the army, they were already experts at both. Boys and girls learned how to use the bow and arrow, as hunting and protecting their herds were essential for survival in the harsh Mongolian environment. This early training made them incredibly strong and precise, preparing them for the demands of war.

The weapon that Mongolian archers used was no ordinary bow. They carried a special type called the composite bow, which was smaller than the longbows used in Europe but much more powerful. Made from layers of wood, animal horn, and sinew, the composite bow was lightweight and flexible, making it perfect for horseback archery. Despite its small size, it could shoot arrows with incredible force and over long distances—up to 350 yards! The bow's design allowed the Mongols to carry it easily and fire quickly, making them deadly opponents on the battlefield.

Mongolian archers also used a variety of arrows, each designed for a specific purpose. Some were heavy and sharp for piercing armor, while others were lighter and used for long-distance attacks. They even had arrows with whistling tips, which made loud noises as they flew through the air. These were used to confuse and intimidate enemies or to send signals during battle. With such a wide range of arrows, Mongolian archers were prepared for any situation they faced.

One of the most remarkable things about Mongolian archers was their ability to shoot accurately while riding at full speed. This required extraordinary balance, coordination, and practice. They developed a unique technique that allowed them to release arrows during the brief moment when all four of their horse's hooves were off the ground. This split-second timing made their shots more stable and accurate. It's no wonder they were considered some of the best horseback archers in history.

The Mongolian army was organized into units of ten, one hundred, one thousand, and ten thousand soldiers, with archers making up a significant portion of these forces. During battle, they used clever tactics to outsmart their enemies. One of their favorite strategies was the "feigned retreat." The Mongols would pretend to flee, luring their enemies into a trap. Once the enemies were off guard, the Mongolian archers would turn around and unleash a deadly rain of arrows, often winning the battle before their opponents even realized what was happening.

The bravery and skill of Mongolian archers weren't limited to battle. They also played an essential role in their communities during times of peace. Hunting with bows and arrows provided food for their families, and archery competitions were a popular activity during festivals. These contests showcased the incredible precision and strength of Mongolian archers, keeping their skills sharp and their spirits high.

The legacy of Mongolian archery goes far beyond the battlefield. The Mongols' mastery of the bow and arrow helped them conquer vast territories, stretching from China to Eastern Europe. Their empire became the largest contiguous land empire in history, connecting people, cultures, and trade routes across the world. The Mongols' ability to adapt their archery skills to different terrains and climates was a key factor in their success. Whether they were fighting in the snowy mountains of Siberia or the deserts of Persia, their archers were always ready to strike with precision and power.

Even after the decline of the Mongol Empire, the traditions of Mongolian archery lived on. Today, archery remains an important part of Mongolian culture. During the annual Naadam Festival, people from across the country gather to compete in archery, wrestling, and horse racing—three traditional sports that showcase the skills of Mongolia's nomadic warriors. Archers at these festivals use bows and arrows similar to those of their ancestors, honoring the legacy of the brave Mongolian archers who once ruled the steppes.

The story of the Mongolian archers is a testament to the power of skill, innovation, and determination. Their ability to combine speed, precision, and strategy made them one of the most formidable forces in history. Whether they were hunting in the wilderness or riding into battle, these warriors carried with them the spirit of Mongolia—strong, fearless, and always aiming for victory. Their legacy continues to inspire people around the world, reminding us of the incredible feats that can be achieved through dedication and courage.

# Chapter 5: Viking Raiders of the North

In the icy, windswept lands of Scandinavia, fierce and adventurous warriors known as the Vikings set out on daring raids that would shape history. These Viking raiders came from what is now Norway, Sweden, and Denmark, and they lived during a time called the Viking Age, which lasted from the late 700s to the early 1100s. They are famous for their fearless voyages across seas, their battles with distant lands, and their enduring spirit of exploration. The Vikings weren't just warriors, though—they were traders, settlers, and skilled craftsmen who left an unforgettable mark on the world.

The word "Viking" comes from the Old Norse word *víkingr*, which means "pirate" or "sea raider." While not all Scandinavians were Vikings, the ones who earned this name were known for their daring raids on coastal towns and monasteries across Europe. These raids began around the year 793, when the Vikings launched a brutal attack on the monastery at Lindisfarne, an island off the coast of England. This event shocked the Christian world and marked the beginning of the Viking Age. Over the next few centuries, Viking raiders became a constant and terrifying presence in Europe.

Vikings were able to travel such great distances thanks to their incredible ships. These ships, called longships, were a marvel of engineering for their time. Long and narrow, with a shallow draft, these vessels could sail across open seas and navigate shallow rivers with ease. They were powered by both sails and oars, making them fast and maneuverable. The longship's design allowed Viking raiders to approach coastal settlements quickly, strike, and retreat before local defenses could respond. Many longships featured dragon-head carvings on their prows, meant to intimidate enemies and protect the ship's crew from evil spirits.

The Viking raiders weren't just about brute force—they were also skilled strategists. Their attacks were carefully planned and often took their enemies by surprise. They targeted isolated villages, wealthy monasteries, and unprotected trade routes. Monasteries were particularly appealing because they were rich in gold, silver, and other treasures, yet poorly defended. The Vikings' ability to strike swiftly and retreat before reinforcements arrived made them nearly unstoppable in their early raids.

Life as a Viking raider was dangerous, but it also offered great rewards. Many Vikings were farmers and fishermen back home, living in harsh conditions with limited resources. Raiding was a way to gain wealth, fame, and a better life for their families. The loot from successful raids included gold, jewels, weapons, and even slaves. These riches helped improve the lives of Viking communities and funded future expeditions. For young warriors, going on a raid was a rite of passage—a chance to prove their courage and skill.

Despite their reputation as ruthless raiders, the Vikings were much more than just pirates. They were also skilled traders who established vast networks that connected Scandinavia with the rest of the world. Viking merchants traveled as far as the Middle East and Central Asia, bringing goods like furs, amber, and walrus ivory to trade for silk, spices, and precious metals. In this way, the Vikings helped spread ideas, cultures, and technologies across great distances, creating a legacy far beyond their raids.

The Vikings were fierce warriors, and their combat skills were honed by their rugged upbringing. From a young age, boys learned to fight with swords, axes, and spears. They also practiced archery and wrestling to build strength and agility. The Viking shield was an essential tool in battle, used not just for defense but also as a weapon. Circular and made of wood, it was lightweight but strong enough to deflect blows. Viking warriors often formed a shield wall in battle, locking their shields together to create a nearly impenetrable barrier. This tactic was both intimidating and highly effective.

The Viking raiders followed the old Norse religion, worshiping gods like Odin, Thor, and Freyja. Odin, the all-father and god of war and wisdom, was especially important to warriors. Vikings believed that dying in battle earned them a place in Valhalla, a grand hall in Asgard where fallen warriors feasted and prepared for Ragnarok, the end of the world. This belief in an honorable death made Viking raiders fearless in combat, as they saw battle as a chance to prove their worth to the gods.

Not all Viking expeditions were about raiding and warfare. Many Vikings also explored and settled in new lands. They established colonies in places like Iceland, Greenland, and even North America, where Leif Erikson and his crew arrived around the year 1000—nearly 500 years before Christopher Columbus. Vikings also settled in parts of England, Scotland, Ireland, and France, where they influenced local cultures and politics. The region of Normandy in France, for example, gets its name from the Norsemen who settled there.

The Viking raiders' influence extended far and wide, leaving behind lasting marks in language, place names, and traditions. Words like "skull," "knife," and "berserk" come from Old Norse, the Vikings' language. Many towns in England have names ending in "-by," like Derby and Whitby, which are derived from Viking settlements. Even today, people in Scandinavian countries celebrate their Viking heritage through festivals, reenactments, and stories.

The Viking Age eventually came to an end in the 11th century. A combination of factors, including stronger defenses in Europe, the spread of Christianity, and the integration of Viking settlers into local populations, led to the decline of raiding. However, the Vikings' legacy continues to captivate imaginations around the world. They are remembered not just as fierce raiders, but as explorers, traders, and innovators who shaped the history of Europe and beyond.

The story of the Viking raiders is one of daring adventure, resilience, and ingenuity. These warriors braved treacherous seas and fierce battles to carve out a place in history, leaving behind tales of bravery and conquest that are still told today. From their fearsome longships to their daring exploits, the Vikings remain legendary figures whose spirit of exploration and determination continues to inspire.

# Chapter 6: Aztec Eagle Warriors

In the grand cities and vast landscapes of ancient Mexico, the Aztec civilization flourished, creating a powerful empire known for its intricate culture, advanced knowledge, and fierce warriors. Among the most respected and skilled fighters in Aztec society were the Eagle Warriors, elite soldiers whose bravery and strength made them legendary. They were not just soldiers; they were symbols of the Aztecs' devotion to their gods, their determination in battle, and their deep connection to nature. These warriors earned their name and status by embodying the qualities of the eagle: sharp-eyed, swift, and fearless.

The Aztec Eagle Warriors were part of a special group of soldiers in the Aztec military, alongside the equally famous Jaguar Warriors. While Jaguar Warriors represented stealth and power on the ground, the Eagle Warriors symbolized the sky, representing the sun and the heavens. They were seen as the warriors of the sun god Huitzilopochtli, who was one of the most important deities in Aztec mythology. The sun god demanded human sacrifices to stay strong and keep the sun moving across the sky, and the Eagle Warriors played a key role in capturing enemies for these rituals.

Becoming an Eagle Warrior was no easy task. Boys in Aztec society began training for warfare at a young age, learning how to use weapons like the macuahuitl, a wooden club embedded with sharp obsidian blades, and the atlatl, a spear-throwing tool. They also practiced using shields and learned strategies to outsmart their enemies. Only those who proved themselves on the battlefield could join the ranks of the Eagle Warriors. One of the most important requirements was capturing enemies alive rather than killing them. This was because the Aztecs valued live captives for their religious sacrifices, which they believed ensured the favor of the gods.

The Eagle Warriors were known for their striking appearance. They wore elaborate costumes designed to resemble eagles, with feathered headdresses, beak-shaped helmets, and cloaks covered in feathers. Their armor was both symbolic and practical, offering protection while intimidating their enemies. The eagle motif was a powerful one in Aztec culture, representing not only strength and vision but also the connection between the earth and the sky. These warriors carried shields decorated with eagle designs and used weapons that reflected their high status, such as intricately crafted macuahuitls.

In battle, the Eagle Warriors were fierce and relentless. They often fought at the front lines, leading Aztec armies into combat. Their goal was not just to defeat their enemies but to capture them alive. This required exceptional skill and bravery, as well as a deep understanding of Aztec warfare tactics. Eagle Warriors worked in coordination with other soldiers, using flanking maneuvers and ambushes to surround their foes. They were also trained in psychological warfare, using loud war cries, drumbeats, and their fearsome appearance to demoralize their enemies.

The Eagle Warriors' bravery extended beyond the battlefield. They were also deeply involved in religious ceremonies, particularly those honoring Huitzilopochtli. After a successful battle, Eagle Warriors participated in rituals to present captured prisoners to the priests. These captives would then be sacrificed in grand ceremonies held at the towering temples of Tenochtitlan, the Aztec capital. The Eagle Warriors believed that their actions helped maintain cosmic order, ensuring that the sun continued to rise and the universe remained in balance.

Being an Eagle Warrior came with great honor and privilege. They were highly respected in Aztec society and enjoyed benefits that ordinary citizens and lower-ranked soldiers did not. For example, Eagle Warriors could wear special clothing that set them apart, eat foods reserved for the nobility, and own land. They also had the opportunity to rise to high-ranking positions in the military or government. Their bravery and dedication were seen as the ultimate expressions of Aztec values, making them role models for the entire civilization.

Despite their strength and skill, the Eagle Warriors and the Aztec Empire faced their greatest challenge in the early 1500s when Spanish conquistadors, led by Hernán Cortés, arrived in Mexico. The Aztecs initially saw the Spanish as powerful but mysterious visitors. However, it soon became clear that the conquistadors sought to conquer their lands. The Aztecs, led by their ruler Montezuma II, fought valiantly against the Spanish forces, with Eagle Warriors playing a central role in the defense of Tenochtitlan.

The Spanish had advanced weapons like firearms and cannons, as well as horses, which the Aztecs had never seen before. Despite this disadvantage, the Eagle Warriors used their knowledge of the terrain and their fearless fighting style to resist the invaders. They fought fiercely in defense of their city and their way of life, but they were ultimately overwhelmed by the Spanish forces and their allies from rival indigenous groups. The fall of Tenochtitlan in 1521 marked the end of the Aztec Empire, but the legacy of the Eagle Warriors endured.

Today, the Eagle Warriors are remembered as symbols of the Aztecs' rich culture, their devotion to their gods, and their unmatched bravery. Their image is celebrated in Mexican art, literature, and festivals, reminding people of the strength and resilience of their ancestors. The story of the Eagle Warriors is a powerful reminder of the importance of courage, loyalty, and the unbreakable bond between people and their beliefs. Though the Aztec Empire is long gone, the spirit of the Eagle Warriors lives on, inspiring generations to honor their history and embrace the qualities that made these ancient warriors legendary.

# Chapter 7: The Shieldmaidens of Legend

In the tales and history of the Viking Age, amidst the icy fjords and rugged landscapes of Scandinavia, there are stories of remarkable women known as Shieldmaidens. These legendary figures were female warriors who stood alongside men in battle, wielding swords, axes, and shields with great skill and bravery. While much of what we know about Shieldmaidens comes from sagas, poems, and legends, their presence has become a symbol of courage, strength, and equality in Viking culture. The Shieldmaidens represent a fascinating part of history where women defied traditional roles to fight for their people and honor.

The Shieldmaidens were not ordinary women; they were extraordinary figures, often described as fierce, independent, and skilled in combat. In Viking society, most women managed households, farms, and families, playing essential roles in everyday life. However, the Shieldmaidens broke this mold, choosing a warrior's life filled with danger and glory. Whether they truly existed as a formal group or were a blend of myth and reality, the stories of Shieldmaidens capture the imagination, showing women as capable fighters who earned respect through their bravery.

To become a Shieldmaiden required training, discipline, and courage. Young Viking girls were taught many skills from an early age, including weaving, cooking, and farming, but some also learned to handle weapons. This was not unusual in Viking culture, where everyone was expected to defend their homes if needed. Shieldmaidens, however, took this training to another level. They practiced swordsmanship, learned how to use shields in combat, and trained to fight in formation. They also developed physical strength and agility, preparing for the challenges of the battlefield. Their shields, often round and made of sturdy wood, were not just defensive tools but symbols of their role as protectors and warriors.

One of the most famous Shieldmaidens in Viking legend is Lagertha, whose story is told in the *Saga of Ragnar Lothbrok*. According to the saga, Lagertha was a fierce warrior who fought alongside the legendary hero Ragnar Lothbrok and later became his wife. She is described as leading troops into battle, her courage and skill inspiring those around her. Another well-known Shieldmaiden is Brynhildr, a figure from Norse mythology who appears in the *Völsunga Saga* and other epic tales. Brynhildr was a Valkyrie, a supernatural being who chose which warriors would live or die in battle, and she exemplified the qualities of strength, wisdom, and independence.

In addition to these legendary figures, archaeological evidence suggests that women in Viking society did sometimes take on warrior roles. One of the most intriguing discoveries is the burial site of a high-ranking Viking warrior in Birka, Sweden. For many years, this grave was assumed to belong to a man because of the weapons, armor, and battle-related items buried with the body. However, modern DNA testing revealed that the warrior was, in fact, a woman. This discovery challenges long-held assumptions about gender roles in Viking society and suggests that women may have been more involved in warfare than previously thought.

The Shieldmaidens were often depicted in Viking sagas as fearless and unwavering, willing to fight for their families, communities, and honor. They participated in battles both large and small, often forming shield walls with their male counterparts. In a shield wall, warriors stood shoulder to shoulder, their shields overlapping to create a nearly impenetrable barrier. This required immense strength, discipline, and trust among the fighters. The Shieldmaidens were also skilled in one-on-one combat, using their weapons with precision and strategy.

In Viking culture, the concept of honor was incredibly important, and this extended to the Shieldmaidens. They fought not just for survival but to uphold the values of their society, including loyalty, bravery, and a deep respect for the gods. Shieldmaidens often swore oaths to serve their leaders or protect their people, and breaking these oaths was considered a grave dishonor. Their dedication to these principles made them both feared and respected on the battlefield.

The Shieldmaidens were also deeply connected to Norse mythology and the spiritual beliefs of the Vikings. They were often associated with the Valkyries, divine maidens who served Odin, the chief of the Norse gods. The Valkyries were said to ride across the skies during battles, choosing which warriors would die and which would be taken to Valhalla, the great hall of the slain. Shieldmaidens, with their courage and combat skills, were seen as mortal counterparts to these divine figures, embodying the same strength and determination.

Although the Viking Age ended centuries ago, the stories of the Shieldmaidens continue to inspire people today. They have become symbols of empowerment, showing that courage and strength are not limited by gender. In modern times, the Shieldmaidens are celebrated in books, movies, and TV shows, where they are portrayed as bold and capable warriors. These depictions honor the spirit of the original legends while reminding us of the power of determination and bravery.

The legacy of the Shieldmaidens extends beyond their stories. They challenge traditional ideas about the roles of women in history and remind us that courage knows no boundaries. Whether they fought in real battles or lived only in the imagination of the Viking storytellers, the Shieldmaidens represent the idea that anyone, regardless of their background, can rise to greatness through skill, dedication, and a fearless heart. Their tales continue to echo through time, inspiring people of all ages to embrace their inner warrior and face life's challenges with strength and resilience.

# Chapter 8: The Courage of the Persian Immortals

In the vast and powerful Persian Empire, one of the most renowned military forces was the Persian Immortals, an elite group of warriors whose skill, discipline, and loyalty made them legendary. They were part of the army of the Achaemenid Empire, which was founded by Cyrus the Great in the 6th century BCE and stretched from the edges of India to the shores of Greece. The Immortals played a vital role in the expansion and defense of this vast empire, earning their name through their unwavering courage and the unique way they were always kept at full strength.

The Persian Immortals were not ordinary soldiers. They were a handpicked force of 10,000 warriors, chosen for their strength, bravery, and loyalty to the king. The name "Immortal" didn't mean they were invincible or lived forever—it came from the fact that their numbers never dropped below 10,000. If a soldier was killed, injured, or retired, he was immediately replaced, giving the impression that the unit was "immortal" in size and strength. This constant replenishment not only ensured the Immortals were always battle-ready but also added to their mystique, making them seem unbeatable to their enemies.

The Immortals were the backbone of the Persian army, serving both as shock troops in battle and as the king's personal guard. They were highly trained in various forms of combat, excelling with weapons like spears, swords, bows, and shields. Their training began at a young age, focusing not only on physical strength but also on discipline and strategy. They were expected to be calm under pressure, follow orders without hesitation, and remain loyal to the empire above all else. This combination of skill and obedience made them a formidable force on the battlefield.

One of the most striking aspects of the Persian Immortals was their appearance. They were known for their elaborate uniforms and weapons, which set them apart from the rest of the army. They wore richly decorated tunics, often adorned with gold and jewels, and carried shields made of wicker, which were lightweight yet effective. Each soldier was armed with a long spear, a bow and arrows, and a short sword for close combat. Their uniformity and splendor not only intimidated their enemies but also showcased the wealth and power of the Persian Empire.

The Immortals were not just warriors—they were also symbols of the king's authority and the unity of the empire. They accompanied the king wherever he went, providing protection and serving as a reminder of his strength. During battles, they often fought at the front lines, leading the charge and inspiring the rest of the army. Their loyalty to the king was absolute, and they were willing to lay down their lives for him without question. This unwavering devotion made them an essential part of the Persian Empire's military and political structure.

One of the most famous moments in the history of the Persian Immortals came during the Greco-Persian Wars, a series of conflicts between the Persian Empire and the city-states of Greece in the 5th century BCE. Under the command of King Xerxes I, the Immortals played a key role in the invasion of Greece. They were part of the massive Persian army that crossed the Hellespont and marched into Greek territory, facing fierce resistance from the Greeks. At the Battle of Thermopylae in 480 BCE, the Immortals fought against the legendary Spartan king Leonidas and his 300 warriors, as well as other Greek allies.

The Battle of Thermopylae is one of the most famous battles in history, and the Immortals were at the center of the action. The Spartans and their allies held a narrow pass against the vastly larger Persian army, using their superior tactics and discipline to inflict heavy losses. The Immortals were sent in to break the Greek defenses, but even they struggled against the determined Spartans. Despite their courage and skill, the Immortals could not overcome the terrain and the Greeks' tight phalanx formation. It was only when a Greek traitor revealed a secret path around the pass that the Persians were able to outflank the Greeks and achieve victory. While the Immortals ultimately triumphed, the fierce resistance of the Spartans made the battle a symbol of bravery and sacrifice.

The Immortals' courage and discipline were not limited to the battlefield. They were also an essential part of Persian society, serving as role models for the rest of the army and the empire. Their presence at royal ceremonies and their role in protecting the king showed the importance of loyalty, unity, and strength in maintaining the empire. The Immortals represented the best of Persian culture, combining martial skill with a deep sense of duty and honor.

The legacy of the Persian Immortals extends far beyond their time. They are remembered as one of the most effective and disciplined military forces of the ancient world. Their example influenced other armies throughout history, inspiring similar elite units in various cultures. The Immortals' commitment to excellence and their unbreakable loyalty to their king and empire continue to symbolize the ideals of courage, unity, and strength.

Today, the Persian Immortals are celebrated as a key part of the rich history of the Persian Empire. Their story is told in history books, movies, and legends, reminding us of their incredible contributions to one of the greatest empires the world has ever known. They were more than just warriors—they were guardians of an empire, symbols of its power, and examples of the extraordinary achievements of the human spirit. The courage of the Persian Immortals lives on, inspiring people to strive for greatness and to stand strong in the face of any challenge.

# Chapter 9: Ancient Egyptian Chariot Riders

In the golden sands and fertile lands of ancient Egypt, a unique and powerful form of warfare emerged: the chariot. While many think of Egypt as the land of pyramids, pharaohs, and temples, it was also a place where innovation in military tactics helped build and protect one of history's greatest civilizations. Among the key players in Egypt's military were the chariot riders, warriors who combined speed, precision, and teamwork to dominate the battlefield. These riders, known as charioteers, were not just soldiers but symbols of power, wealth, and the might of the Egyptian pharaohs.

The use of chariots in Egypt began during the Second Intermediate Period (around 1650–1550 BCE) when the Hyksos, a foreign people who ruled parts of northern Egypt, introduced the Egyptians to this revolutionary war machine. The Egyptians quickly adopted and improved upon the chariot, turning it into a weapon of extraordinary efficiency. By the time of the New Kingdom (around 1550–1070 BCE), chariots had become a cornerstone of Egyptian military strategy, playing a crucial role in the empire's expansion and defense.

An Egyptian chariot was a lightweight, two-wheeled vehicle made primarily of wood and leather. It was designed for speed and maneuverability, allowing it to dart across the battlefield with ease. The wheels were spoked, reducing weight, and the body was reinforced with leather bindings for durability. The chariot was typically pulled by two horses, which were highly trained for both speed and stamina. These horses were bred and cared for with great attention, as they were seen as vital members of the army. A team of charioteers consisted of two people: the driver, who controlled the horses, and the warrior, who wielded weapons such as bows, spears, and javelins.

Charioteers underwent rigorous training to master their roles. Driving a chariot required exceptional skill, as the driver had to maintain control of the horses while navigating the chaos of battle. This involved not only steering but also maintaining the balance of the chariot over uneven terrain. The warrior, meanwhile, trained in archery and spear-throwing, often practicing to hit moving targets while the chariot raced at full speed. The combination of a skilled driver and an accurate archer made the Egyptian chariot an incredibly effective weapon. The teamwork between the two charioteers was essential; they had to trust each other completely to survive and succeed in battle.

The role of chariot riders extended beyond combat. They were also responsible for scouting and reconnaissance, using their speed to gather information about enemy movements and terrain. This intelligence was crucial for planning strategies and preparing for battle. Charioteers also served as messengers, delivering orders quickly across the battlefield. In peacetime, chariots were used in royal ceremonies and processions, where their speed and elegance symbolized the power and authority of the pharaoh. Some chariots were even elaborately decorated with gold and precious stones, serving as symbols of wealth and prestige.

One of the most famous battles involving Egyptian chariot riders was the Battle of Kadesh in 1274 BCE, fought between the forces of Pharaoh Ramesses II and the Hittite king Muwatalli II. This battle, one of the largest chariot battles in history, showcased the strategic importance of chariots in ancient warfare. Ramesses II led his army, which included thousands of chariots, into the fray against the Hittites, who also had a formidable chariot corps. The battle was intense, with both sides using their chariots to outflank and charge at each other. Although the battle ended in a stalemate, it demonstrated the skill and courage of the Egyptian charioteers, who were instrumental in preventing a decisive defeat.

The life of an Egyptian charioteer was both dangerous and rewarding. These warriors faced incredible risks on the battlefield, where a single mistake could mean death. Yet, they were also highly respected and often rewarded for their bravery and skill. Successful charioteers could rise to prominent positions in the military or even the royal court. They were often depicted in tomb paintings and temple reliefs, immortalized for their heroism and contributions to the empire.

The importance of chariots in Egyptian society went beyond their military use. They represented the technological and cultural advancements of the civilization, showcasing the ingenuity and adaptability of the Egyptians. Chariots were also tied to the divine, often associated with the sun god Ra, who was said to ride across the sky in a chariot. This connection to the gods elevated the status of charioteers, making them not just warriors but sacred figures in the eyes of the people.

As time went on, changes in warfare and technology led to the decline of the chariot's dominance. The rise of cavalry, which provided greater flexibility and speed, eventually made chariots less effective on the battlefield. However, the legacy of the Egyptian chariot riders lived on, remembered as pioneers of ancient military strategy and symbols of the might of the pharaohs. Their courage, skill, and dedication remain a fascinating chapter in the story of ancient Egypt.

Even today, the story of the Egyptian charioteers continues to inspire and intrigue. They were more than just soldiers; they were innovators, leaders, and heroes who played a pivotal role in the rise and glory of one of the ancient world's greatest civilizations. Their chariots, racing across the sands of history, remind us of the incredible achievements of ancient Egypt and the courage of those who defended its lands and people.

# Chapter 10: Mayan Warriors in Battle

In the lush jungles and vast plains of Mesoamerica, the Maya civilization thrived for thousands of years, creating advanced cities, towering temples, and a complex culture deeply rooted in religion, art, and science. But the Maya were not just scholars and architects; they were also fierce warriors. Their armies fought to expand their kingdoms, defend their cities, and maintain their power. Mayan warriors were experts in battle, employing clever strategies, unique weapons, and a deep connection to their gods and leaders. Their story is one of courage, skill, and devotion, shaped by the challenges of the rugged land and the rivalries of their powerful city-states.

Mayan warriors were not part of a single empire, as the Maya civilization was made up of independent city-states like Tikal, Calakmul, Copán, and Palenque. These cities often competed for control of resources, trade routes, and land, leading to frequent battles. Warfare was not just about conquest; it was also deeply connected to Mayan religion and politics. Warriors fought to capture enemies for sacrifices to the gods, demonstrate their ruler's strength, and protect the honor of their city. This made the role of a warrior one of the most respected and dangerous positions in Mayan society.

The training of a Mayan warrior began early, especially for the sons of nobles, who were expected to lead armies and protect their people. These young men were taught the skills of archery, spear-throwing, and hand-to-hand combat. They practiced using a tool called the *atlatl*, a spear-thrower that allowed them to hurl darts with great speed and accuracy. They also learned to wield the *macuahuitl*, a wooden club edged with sharp obsidian blades, capable of inflicting devastating injuries. Commoners could also join the ranks of warriors, especially during times of war, but their training was less formal. Still, every warrior was expected to show courage and loyalty, as defeat or capture could bring great shame to their city.

A Mayan warrior's appearance was as fierce as his skills. Before battle, warriors adorned themselves with elaborate costumes designed to intimidate their enemies and honor their gods. They painted their bodies with bright colors like red, black, and yellow, often using symbols that represented their totem animals or deities. Many wore fearsome headdresses made of feathers, animal skins, or even carved wooden masks, transforming them into jaguars, eagles, or other powerful creatures. Jaguar warriors, for example, were elite fighters who symbolized strength and stealth, while eagle warriors represented speed and vision. These animal spirits were believed to give the warriors special powers in battle.

The weapons of the Mayan warriors were both deadly and beautifully crafted. The *macuahuitl*, made of hardwood and obsidian, could cut through flesh and armor with ease. They also used spears tipped with obsidian or flint, bows and arrows, and slings for long-range attacks. For close combat, they carried small knives and axes. The *atlatl* was particularly important, as it allowed warriors to strike from a distance with remarkable precision. In addition to weapons, warriors carried shields made of wood or woven reeds, often decorated with bright patterns or animal symbols. These shields provided protection while adding to the warrior's striking appearance.

Mayan battles were carefully planned and often began with rituals and ceremonies. Before going to war, leaders would consult the gods through divination, seeking signs of favor or warning. Warriors participated in religious rites, offering blood sacrifices to ensure victory. When the time came to march, the army moved through the jungle in organized groups, led by nobles or war captains. They communicated with whistles, drums, and conch shells, using specific rhythms to signal commands or coordinate attacks. These sounds, combined with the warriors' fierce cries, created an overwhelming noise meant to terrify their enemies.

On the battlefield, Mayan warfare was a mix of strategy, agility, and brute force. The thick jungles and uneven terrain of Mesoamerica required warriors to be highly mobile and adaptable. They used ambush tactics, striking quickly and then retreating into the forest to confuse and weaken their opponents. When armies met in open combat, formations were key, with warriors advancing in rows while archers and slingers attacked from a distance. Leaders played a crucial role, inspiring their troops with bravery and directing their movements to exploit weaknesses in the enemy's defenses.

One of the most important goals of Mayan warfare was to capture prisoners, especially enemy nobles and warriors of high rank. These captives were taken back to the victor's city, where they were often sacrificed to honor the gods. The capture of a powerful enemy was considered a great achievement, bringing prestige to the warrior and his city. For the Maya, this act of sacrifice was not seen as cruelty but as a sacred duty, ensuring the balance of the universe and the favor of the gods.

While warfare was common among the Maya, it also had devastating consequences. Cities were destroyed, populations were displaced, and resources were depleted. Over time, this constant fighting may have contributed to the decline of the Maya civilization, as rivalries and invasions weakened the once-great city-states. Despite this, the legacy of the Mayan warriors lives on, remembered for their bravery, skill, and devotion to their culture and gods.

Today, the story of the Mayan warriors is told through the ruins of their cities, the intricate carvings on their monuments, and the myths passed down through generations. These warriors were not just fighters; they were protectors of a civilization, defenders of their beliefs, and symbols of the strength and resilience of the Maya people. Their courage and dedication remind us of the challenges they faced and the incredible achievements of one of history's most remarkable cultures.

# Chapter 11: The Fearless Zulu Fighters

In the heart of southern Africa, among rolling hills and vast grasslands, a proud and powerful people known as the Zulu rose to prominence. Their name would become synonymous with courage, resilience, and unmatched skill in battle. The Zulu fighters, or warriors, were central to the growth and defense of the Zulu Kingdom, which reached its peak under the leadership of King Shaka Zulu in the early 19th century. Their story is one of strategy, innovation, and fearless determination, as they defended their land and people against rival tribes, European colonizers, and any force that threatened their way of life.

Zulu warriors were not just soldiers; they were part of a deeply structured society where every man was expected to serve his community and king. From a young age, Zulu boys were prepared for a life of discipline and combat. They grew up in tightly knit homesteads, learning the values of loyalty, teamwork, and respect for their elders. As soon as they were old enough, they joined *ibutho*—age-based military regiments that formed the backbone of the Zulu army. These regiments were more than fighting units; they were brotherhoods where young men forged bonds and learned the skills they would need to protect their people.

Shaka Zulu, one of the most brilliant military leaders in history, transformed the Zulu army into a fearsome force. Before his reign, battles between tribes were often symbolic, with minimal casualties and an emphasis on displays of bravery. Shaka changed this approach entirely, introducing tactics and innovations that prioritized victory. He reorganized the army into disciplined formations, trained his warriors rigorously, and developed new weapons that revolutionized Zulu warfare.

One of Shaka's most famous innovations was the *iklwa*, a short stabbing spear that replaced the traditional long throwing spear. The *iklwa* was designed for close combat, allowing warriors to engage their enemies more effectively. Shaka also introduced a large, oval-shaped shield made from cowhide. These shields provided excellent protection and were used not only to block attacks but also to maneuver opponents in battle. The combination of the *iklwa* and the shield gave Zulu warriors a significant advantage in close-quarters combat, making them almost unstoppable in hand-to-hand fights.

Shaka's tactical genius extended to the way he organized his armies on the battlefield. He developed the famous "horns of the buffalo" formation, a strategy that involved dividing the army into three groups. The "chest" formed the main force, engaging the enemy head-on, while the "horns" flanked the opponent, encircling them and cutting off any escape routes. The "loins," or reserve force, stayed behind, ready to reinforce the chest or pursue fleeing enemies. This approach was both innovative and devastatingly effective, allowing the Zulu to outmaneuver and overwhelm their enemies time and again.

Zulu warriors were known for their incredible stamina and speed. They trained relentlessly, often running barefoot across rough terrain to build their endurance. They could march great distances quickly, giving them the ability to surprise their enemies with sudden attacks. Their physical conditioning, combined with their discipline and unity, made them one of the most formidable fighting forces of their time.

Despite their focus on battle, the Zulu fighters were also deeply connected to their culture and traditions. Before going to war, they participated in ceremonies and rituals to seek the blessings of their ancestors and spirits. These rituals included dances, chants, and sacrifices, all designed to strengthen their resolve and ensure the favor of the gods. The warriors believed that their courage and skill in battle were tied to their spiritual strength, which they drew from their connection to their community and their ancestors.

One of the most famous moments in Zulu history was the Battle of Isandlwana in 1879, during the Anglo-Zulu War. At this battle, the Zulu army, armed mostly with traditional weapons, faced the British, who had modern rifles and artillery. Despite being outgunned, the Zulu warriors displayed extraordinary bravery and tactical skill. Using their "horns of the buffalo" formation, they surrounded the British forces and inflicted one of the greatest defeats ever suffered by a colonial army in Africa. The victory at Isandlwana shocked the world and demonstrated the incredible capabilities of the Zulu fighters.

However, the Zulu faced many challenges in the years that followed. The British, determined to conquer the Zulu Kingdom, launched a massive campaign to defeat them. Despite their bravery and determination, the Zulu were eventually overwhelmed by the superior firepower and resources of the British Empire. The fall of the Zulu Kingdom marked the end of an era, but the legacy of the Zulu warriors endured.

The Zulu fighters were more than just soldiers; they were protectors of their land, their people, and their traditions. Their courage and skill in battle were matched by their dedication to their culture and their king. They fought not only with weapons but with their hearts, believing that their strength came from their unity and their connection to their ancestors. Even in defeat, they remained a symbol of resistance and resilience, inspiring future generations to honor their heritage.

Today, the story of the fearless Zulu fighters is celebrated as a testament to the power of discipline, innovation, and community. Their contributions to history are remembered not only in South Africa but around the world, where their name stands as a symbol of courage and strength. The Zulu warriors remind us that even against overwhelming odds, bravery and unity can achieve extraordinary things. Their legacy lives on in the hearts of their descendants, who continue to honor the spirit of the fearless Zulu fighters.

# Chapter 12: Celtic Warriors and Their Painted Faces

In the misty hills, deep forests, and rugged landscapes of ancient Europe, the Celts flourished as a vibrant and powerful people. Known for their artistry, rich mythology, and fierce independence, the Celts were also renowned warriors. Among their many striking features was their practice of painting their faces and bodies before battle, a tradition that set them apart and added an almost mythical aura to their reputation. These warriors, hailing from regions that now include Ireland, Scotland, Wales, and parts of mainland Europe, were not just fighters—they were protectors of their clans and defenders of their land and traditions.

The Celts were not a single, unified group but a collection of tribes that shared similar languages, culture, and beliefs. Each tribe had its own leaders and warriors, and conflicts between tribes were common. At the same time, they were bound by shared traditions, including their approach to warfare. For the Celts, battle was more than just a test of strength; it was an expression of their identity, bravery, and spiritual connection to the natural world. Their painted faces and bodies were a key part of this expression, turning each warrior into a living symbol of their culture.

One of the most fascinating aspects of Celtic warriors was their use of body paint, particularly a blue dye made from the *woad* plant. The process of creating this dye was intricate, involving boiling the leaves of the woad plant to extract the pigment. Once prepared, the warriors applied the dye in swirling, intricate patterns across their skin. These designs were not random; they held symbolic meanings, often representing the gods, nature, or the warrior's personal or clan identity. The paint wasn't just for decoration—it was also believed to have protective qualities, both spiritual and physical. Warriors thought it might bring them the favor of the gods or even frighten away their enemies.

The painted designs served another important purpose: intimidation. Imagine a line of warriors, their faces and bodies covered in swirling blue patterns, standing tall and shouting battle cries as they prepared to charge. To their enemies, this sight was terrifying, almost otherworldly. The Celts understood the psychological power of appearance, and their painted faces were as much a weapon as their swords, spears, and shields. The bright, bold patterns caught the light and made the warriors look larger than life, creating an impression of invincibility.

Celtic warriors were famous for their ferocity and skill in battle. They fought with a wide range of weapons, including long swords, spears, and axes, many of which were beautifully crafted and decorated. Their shields, often made of wood and reinforced with metal, were not only functional but also artistic, adorned with intricate designs. Some warriors fought with little or no armor, relying on their speed, agility, and courage. This daring approach to combat added to their fearsome reputation, as they seemed to have no fear of injury or death.

The Celts were deeply spiritual, and their warfare was closely tied to their beliefs. They saw the world as a place filled with spirits, gods, and forces of nature, and they believed that battle was a sacred act. Before going to war, Celtic warriors often participated in rituals and ceremonies led by the druids, who were the spiritual leaders of their society. These rituals included prayers, sacrifices, and blessings meant to ensure victory and protection. The warriors carried these blessings into battle, feeling empowered and connected to their gods and ancestors.

One of the most iconic symbols of Celtic warriors was their long hair and mustaches. Many warriors wore their hair in elaborate styles, sometimes stiffened with lime to create striking shapes. Combined with their painted faces and fierce expressions, this added to their imposing appearance. These hairstyles and body art were a way to stand out, not just on the battlefield but within their tribes, as warriors were often celebrated for their bravery and individuality.

Celtic warfare was not just about brute strength; it also involved clever tactics and strategies. The Celts were masters of ambushes and guerrilla warfare, using their knowledge of the land to their advantage. They often lured enemies into forests or narrow valleys where larger armies couldn't maneuver effectively. Their chariots, pulled by swift and sturdy horses, were another key part of their strategy. These chariots allowed them to strike quickly and retreat just as fast, keeping their enemies off balance.

While the Celts were known for their independence and internal conflicts, they also faced external threats. Roman writers, such as Julius Caesar, documented encounters with Celtic tribes during the Roman Empire's expansion. The Celts' painted warriors made a lasting impression on the Romans, who described their bravery, ferocity, and unique appearance. Although the Romans eventually conquered many Celtic territories, the Celts resisted fiercely, with some tribes continuing to fight long after their lands had been taken.

One of the most famous examples of Celtic resistance was the rebellion led by Boudicca, the warrior queen of the Iceni tribe, in what is now Britain. Boudicca's army, likely including many painted warriors, fought valiantly against the Romans, inflicting heavy losses before eventually being defeated. Her story became a symbol of Celtic courage and the determination to defend their way of life.

The painted warriors of the Celts left an enduring legacy. Their boldness in battle, their connection to their spiritual beliefs, and their artistic expressions through body paint and design captured the imagination of those who encountered them. Even today, the image of a Celtic warrior, standing tall with painted face and fierce eyes, remains a powerful symbol of courage, independence, and the enduring spirit of a people who refused to be forgotten.

As we look back on the history of the Celtic warriors, we see not just fighters but also artists, leaders, and protectors of a vibrant culture. Their painted faces were more than decoration; they were a statement of who they were and what they stood for—a reminder that bravery comes in many forms, and sometimes, the most striking armor is the spirit within. The legacy of the Celtic warriors lives on in the stories, symbols, and traditions of the descendants of this remarkable people.

# Chapter 13: The Knights of Medieval Europe

In the grand castles and battlefields of medieval Europe, knights stood as symbols of honor, bravery, and chivalry. These armored warriors were the backbone of feudal armies, sworn to serve their lords and protect their lands. Knights were not just soldiers; they were part of a complex and romanticized tradition that defined the Middle Ages. Their training, weapons, codes of conduct, and dramatic role in history make their story a fascinating glimpse into a world of castles, kings, and epic battles.

Knighthood was not something that anyone could achieve easily. It was reserved for boys born into noble families, as their wealth and status were necessary to afford the training, weapons, and armor required to become a knight. From a young age, a boy destined for knighthood would begin his journey as a page. Starting around the age of seven, pages lived in the castle of a lord or knight, where they learned the basics of courtly life and the early skills of combat. They were taught to ride horses, handle small weapons, and serve their superiors with respect and loyalty. They also received an education in reading, writing, and the principles of Christianity, which were deeply tied to the idea of knighthood.

Around the age of 14, a page would advance to the rank of squire. As a squire, the young nobleman became a knight's personal assistant and apprentice. He would care for the knight's armor and weapons, help him prepare for battle, and accompany him on campaigns. This hands-on experience was crucial, as it gave the squire a chance to observe and learn the realities of combat. Squires also continued their training, practicing with swords, shields, and lances, and honing their skills in tournaments and mock battles. By the time a squire was in his late teens or early twenties, he could be knighted, provided he had demonstrated the courage, skill, and honor expected of a knight.

The knighting ceremony was a grand and solemn event, often held in a church or castle. It began with the squire spending the night in prayer, asking for guidance and strength from God. The next day, he would bathe and dress in a white tunic, symbolizing purity, and a red cloak, representing his readiness to shed blood for his lord and faith. A priest would bless him, and then a lord or knight would perform the act of dubbing, touching the squire's shoulders with a sword and declaring him a knight. From that moment, the new knight was bound by the chivalric code—a set of moral and social rules that emphasized loyalty, bravery, and courtesy.

The code of chivalry was central to a knight's identity. While the exact details of the code varied, it generally required knights to be loyal to their lord and king, protect the weak, defend the church, and act honorably in all things. Knights were expected to show mercy to their enemies, treat women with respect, and remain humble despite their power. In reality, not all knights lived up to these ideals, but the code of chivalry became a powerful symbol of what knights aspired to be. It also gave rise to the romantic image of the knight as a noble hero, which has endured in literature and legend.

Knights were equipped with some of the most advanced and impressive gear of their time. Their suits of armor, made of interlocking metal plates or chainmail, provided excellent protection while allowing enough mobility for combat. Helmets, gauntlets, and shields added extra layers of defense. The weapons of a knight were both practical and symbolic. The sword, often the most prized possession of a knight, represented strength and justice. Knights also wielded lances for mounted combat, axes for close fighting, and daggers as a last resort. Their warhorses, trained for battle, were as much a part of their arsenal as any weapon, capable of charging into enemy lines with tremendous force.

Knights were primarily mounted warriors, and their horses played a vital role in their success. These steeds were bred and trained specifically for battle, capable of carrying a fully armored knight at high speeds and remaining calm amidst the chaos of combat. Knights and their horses formed a powerful unit on the battlefield, with their charges capable of breaking through enemy lines. This combination of man and horse was so effective that it defined European warfare for centuries.

In addition to real battles, knights participated in tournaments, which were a mix of sport and training. These events included jousting, where knights charged at each other with lances in an attempt to unseat their opponent, and melee battles, where groups of knights fought in mock combat. Tournaments were not only a way to practice combat skills but also a chance to win fame and fortune. Victorious knights could earn the admiration of nobles and commoners alike, as well as valuable prizes or ransoms from defeated opponents.

Knights were not only warriors but also defenders of their lords' estates. During times of peace, they acted as enforcers of the law, protectors of villagers, and representatives of their lord's authority. They also participated in the construction and defense of castles, which served as both fortresses and symbols of power. When a castle was under siege, knights played a crucial role in its defense, using their skills and strategies to hold off attackers.

The era of knights reached its height during the medieval period, roughly from the 9th to the 15th centuries. However, changes in technology and society eventually brought about the decline of knighthood. The invention of gunpowder and firearms made heavily armored knights less effective on the battlefield, while the rise of professional armies reduced the reliance on feudal lords and their knights. By the late Middle Ages, the romantic image of the knight had largely replaced their practical role as warriors.

Even as their role in warfare faded, the legacy of knights endured. Their ideals of chivalry, bravery, and honor continued to inspire stories, poems, and traditions. Tales of King Arthur and the Knights of the Round Table, though largely fictional, captured the imagination of generations and kept the spirit of knighthood alive. The image of a knight in shining armor, riding into battle or rescuing those in need, remains a powerful symbol of heroism to this day.

The story of the knights of medieval Europe is a rich tapestry of history, myth, and culture. They were not only warriors but also symbols of a time when loyalty, courage, and honor were held in the highest regard. Their legacy, immortalized in countless legends and traditions, reminds us of a fascinating chapter in human history—a time when men in shining armor rode out to fight for their lords, their faith, and their dreams of glory.

# Chapter 14: Amazon Warriors of Myth

The Amazon warriors are among the most legendary figures of ancient mythology, often described as fierce, fearless women who defied the traditional roles of their time to become some of the most skilled and powerful fighters in history. Their stories have been passed down through generations in Greek mythology, capturing imaginations with tales of their courage, independence, and determination. While their existence is shrouded in myth, the Amazons have become enduring symbols of strength and resilience, inspiring countless tales, artworks, and interpretations.

According to legend, the Amazons were a race of warrior women who lived in a society that excluded men from leadership roles. They were believed to inhabit a distant land, often described as Scythia near the Black Sea or regions even farther away, such as the fringes of Asia. The Greeks envisioned their homeland as a place of rugged beauty, surrounded by forests, rivers, and mountains. In this society, women were the rulers, hunters, and warriors, while men played minor roles or were excluded altogether. This reversal of traditional gender roles was a central aspect of the Amazon myth, making them both fascinating and controversial figures in ancient stories.

The Amazons were said to be exceptional fighters, trained in the arts of war from a young age. They were masters of archery, skilled with spears, and highly adept at horseback riding, often attacking with swift and precise movements. Their connection to horses and mobility in battle set them apart from other warriors of their time. The bow and arrow were their signature weapons, and they were believed to be able to shoot with deadly accuracy, even while riding at full speed. Their strength, agility, and tactical brilliance allowed them to defeat many male opponents, earning them a reputation as nearly invincible on the battlefield.

One of the most famous myths involving the Amazons is the story of their queen, Hippolyta. According to Greek legend, Hippolyta possessed a magical girdle (a kind of belt) given to her by the god of war, Ares. This girdle symbolized her authority and power as the queen of the Amazons. In one tale, Heracles (known to the Romans as Hercules) was tasked with retrieving this girdle as one of his Twelve Labors. When Heracles arrived in the land of the Amazons, Hippolyta initially agreed to give him the girdle willingly. However, the goddess Hera, jealous and determined to cause trouble, spread rumors that Heracles intended to harm the queen. This misunderstanding led to a fierce battle between Heracles and the Amazons, resulting in Hippolyta's death in some versions of the story.

The Amazons also appear in the legend of the Trojan War, where they fought alongside the Trojans against the Greeks. The Amazon queen Penthesilea, another prominent figure in their mythology, led her warriors into battle with unmatched bravery. Penthesilea is often portrayed as a tragic hero, skilled in combat but doomed by fate. During the war, she faced the Greek hero Achilles in single combat. Though she fought valiantly, Achilles ultimately killed her. According to some versions of the story, Achilles was struck by her beauty and mourned her death, adding a layer of complexity to the tale and highlighting the respect the Amazons commanded, even among their enemies.

Another fascinating aspect of Amazonian mythology is their connection to the gods and the natural world. The Amazons were often portrayed as deeply spiritual, with a strong reverence for the deities of war, hunting, and the wilderness. They were sometimes associated with Artemis, the goddess of the hunt and protector of women. Like Artemis, the Amazons were depicted as independent, resourceful, and deeply in tune with nature. Their lifestyle, focused on self-reliance and martial prowess, reflected these values, emphasizing their unique position as both warriors and protectors of their land.

The Amazons' relationship with men in myth is complex and often contradictory. While they were known for their independence and avoidance of traditional relationships, some stories describe them as engaging with men to ensure the continuation of their society. According to one myth, the Amazons would visit neighboring tribes to have children, keeping the girls to raise as warriors and sending the boys back to their fathers or leaving them in the care of other tribes. This aspect of their mythology underscores their dedication to maintaining a society centered on female strength and autonomy.

The origin of the Amazon myth has intrigued historians and scholars for centuries. Some believe that the stories of the Amazons may have been inspired by real-life warrior women from ancient cultures. For example, the Scythians, a nomadic people who lived in the steppes of Central Asia, included women who fought alongside men in battle. Archaeological evidence, such as graves containing weapons alongside the remains of women, suggests that these warrior women could have inspired the Greek tales of the Amazons. While we may never know for certain, this connection between myth and history adds another layer of intrigue to their story.

The Amazons were not without their critics in ancient Greek culture. Some Greeks viewed them as a threat to the established social order, representing a world turned upside down where women ruled and men were subservient. This fear of the Amazons was often reflected in their portrayal as fierce and sometimes savage warriors who needed to be subdued by male heroes. At the same time, they were admired for their courage and strength, embodying qualities that even their opponents respected.

Over time, the image of the Amazon has evolved, taking on new meanings in different contexts. In medieval Europe, they were often reinterpreted as exotic figures in chivalric tales. In modern times, the Amazons have become symbols of female empowerment and independence, celebrated in literature, film, and popular culture.

Characters like Wonder Woman, who draws inspiration from Amazonian mythology, have brought their legacy to new audiences, emphasizing their timeless appeal as warriors who defied expectations and fought for their ideals.

The Amazons' story, whether rooted in myth, history, or a blend of both, continues to captivate and inspire. Their fierce independence, dedication to their people, and unwavering courage remind us of the power of resilience and determination. Whether imagined as mythical figures or as echoes of real-life warrior women, the Amazons stand as enduring symbols of strength and the unbreakable spirit of those who dare to forge their own path.

# Chapter 15: The Guardians of the Great Wall

The story of the guardians of the Great Wall of China is a tale of resilience, strategy, and determination that spans centuries. These men and women dedicated their lives to protecting one of the most extraordinary structures ever built, a massive wall that snakes across thousands of miles, hugging mountain ridges, cutting through valleys, and stretching into deserts. The Great Wall was not just a barrier of stone and brick; it was a lifeline for the Chinese empire, a symbol of strength, and a testament to the ingenuity and perseverance of its builders and defenders.

The origins of the Great Wall can be traced back over 2,000 years, during the time of the Warring States period (475–221 BCE). Back then, China was not a unified empire but a collection of feuding states. Each of these states built its own walls to protect against invasions from neighboring rivals and nomadic tribes. When Emperor Qin Shi Huang, the first emperor of a united China, came to power in 221 BCE, he ordered these individual walls to be connected and expanded, creating the foundation for what would eventually become the Great Wall of China. This immense task required countless workers, including soldiers, peasants, and even convicts, who toiled day and night to build this defensive masterpiece.

As the wall grew, so did the need for guardians to defend it. The primary purpose of the Great Wall was to protect the Chinese empire from invasions by nomadic tribes, particularly the Xiongnu, who were skilled horsemen and fierce warriors from the northern steppes. These invaders would often raid Chinese settlements, stealing livestock, crops, and wealth. The guardians of the wall were the first line of defense against these attacks, stationed in watchtowers and fortresses strategically placed along the wall's length. These soldiers were not just warriors but also scouts, messengers, and caretakers of the wall itself.

Life as a guardian of the Great Wall was not easy. The soldiers endured harsh conditions, from the scorching heat of summer to the freezing winds of winter. The Great Wall stretches across a variety of terrains, including mountains, deserts, and plains, and the guardians had to adapt to the unique challenges of each region. They lived in barracks near the wall, often far from their families, with limited supplies and resources. Despite these hardships, the guardians were expected to remain vigilant at all times, watching for signs of enemy movements and ready to sound the alarm if danger approached.

One of the most critical roles of the wall's guardians was manning the watchtowers, which served as lookout points, communication hubs, and defensive strongholds. These towers were spaced at regular intervals along the wall, allowing soldiers to see long distances and relay messages quickly. If enemy forces were spotted, the guardians would light signal fires made from wood and straw during the day or use torches at night to warn nearby garrisons. This system of communication allowed reinforcements to be mobilized rapidly, creating a coordinated defense that could stretch across vast distances.

The guardians of the Great Wall were also responsible for maintaining the wall itself. This was no small task, as the wall was constantly exposed to the elements and required regular repairs. Erosion, harsh weather, and attacks from invaders could damage the structure, and the guardians worked alongside laborers to keep it in good condition. The materials used to build the wall varied depending on the region, ranging from tamped earth and wood in some areas to bricks and stone in others. Guardians needed to be resourceful, using whatever materials were available to ensure the wall remained strong and secure.

Over the centuries, the Great Wall saw many battles and skirmishes, and the guardians played a crucial role in defending the empire. One of the most famous confrontations occurred during the Ming Dynasty

(1368–1644), when the Great Wall was rebuilt and fortified to protect against the Mongols. The Mongol Empire, led by Genghis Khan and later his descendants, had previously conquered China, establishing the Yuan Dynasty (1271–1368). When the Chinese overthrew the Mongols and established the Ming Dynasty, they sought to prevent another invasion by strengthening the Great Wall and stationing more guardians along its length.

The Ming-era guardians were highly organized, with a military system that divided the wall into sections, each overseen by a commander. Soldiers stationed at the wall underwent rigorous training in archery, swordsmanship, and hand-to-hand combat. They were also skilled in the use of early firearms, such as matchlock muskets and cannons, which gave them an advantage against their enemies. Despite these advancements, defending the wall remained a daunting task, as the nomadic tribes of the north were relentless in their attempts to breach it.

One of the most famous sections of the Great Wall is the Jiayuguan Pass, located at the westernmost end of the Ming-era wall. This pass was heavily fortified and served as a key entry point into China. The guardians stationed here were responsible for monitoring trade caravans traveling along the Silk Road, ensuring the safety of merchants and preventing smuggling or unauthorized entry. The guardians at Jiayuguan played a dual role as both protectors and gatekeepers, managing the flow of people and goods into the empire.

The guardians of the Great Wall were not always professional soldiers. In times of peace, local villagers and farmers often took on the role of defending the wall. These citizen-soldiers were trained by military leaders and called upon when needed. They were familiar with the surrounding terrain, making them effective scouts and defenders. In return for their service, these guardians were sometimes granted land or tax exemptions, providing them with a modest reward for their efforts.

Despite the dedication of its guardians, the Great Wall was not invincible. In 1644, the Manchu forces of the Qing Dynasty were able to bypass the wall by allying with a disloyal general who opened the gates at the Shanhai Pass, allowing them to conquer China. This marked the end of the Ming Dynasty and the beginning of Qing rule. Although the wall could not prevent all invasions, its presence slowed down enemies, provided strategic advantages, and became a powerful symbol of China's determination to defend its people and culture.

Today, the Great Wall stands as one of the most iconic landmarks in the world, a testament to the ingenuity and perseverance of ancient China. The legacy of its guardians lives on in the stories of their courage and dedication. While the wall no longer serves as a military fortification, it remains a source of pride and inspiration, reminding us of the incredible achievements of those who built and defended it. The guardians of the Great Wall were more than soldiers—they were protectors of a civilization, standing watch over one of the greatest architectural feats in human history.

# Chapter 16: Native American Bravehearts

Native American Bravehearts were the courageous warriors of the many Indigenous tribes across North America, who fought not only to protect their people but also to defend their culture, lands, and way of life. These warriors embodied bravery, skill, and deep spiritual connection, acting as protectors and role models within their communities. Their stories, passed down through oral traditions, are tales of resilience, sacrifice, and an unbreakable bond with the land they called home. Every tribe had its own traditions, but all shared a profound respect for the warrior's role as both a fighter and a guardian of their people.

In Native American cultures, becoming a warrior was not just about learning how to fight; it was about embodying values like courage, honor, and selflessness. From a young age, boys were taught the skills they would need to survive and protect their people. They learned to hunt, track animals, and move silently through forests, plains, or mountains. These skills were essential for providing food for the tribe, but they also became vital in times of conflict. Training often included tests of endurance, where boys had to endure cold, hunger, or pain without complaint, teaching them to remain strong and focused in the face of hardship.

The weapons of Native American Bravehearts varied by region and resources, reflecting the diverse environments in which they lived. Tribes in the Great Plains, such as the Lakota or Cheyenne, were skilled horsemen and often used bows and arrows or spears in battle. Their bows were expertly crafted from wood and sinew, making them lightweight yet powerful. These warriors also carried tomahawks, which could be used for close combat or thrown with remarkable accuracy. Tribes in wooded areas, like the Iroquois, used longbows and war clubs, while those in the Southwest, such as the Apache, relied on knives, slings, and later, firearms acquired through trade or conflict with European settlers.

The role of the warrior extended beyond the battlefield. Bravehearts were seen as protectors of their tribe's traditions, values, and sacred sites.

They participated in ceremonies and rituals that connected them to the spiritual world, seeking guidance and strength from their ancestors and the spirits of nature. Before going into battle, warriors would often perform rituals to prepare themselves mentally and spiritually. This might involve painting their bodies with symbols of protection or strength, singing songs of courage, or seeking visions through fasting and prayer. These practices reinforced their connection to the land and their belief that they were fighting for more than just survival—they were defending the soul of their people.

Warriors also carried with them symbols of their bravery and achievements. Feathers, especially from eagles, were highly prized and often worn in headdresses or tied to weapons. Each feather represented a specific act of courage or skill, such as striking an enemy in battle or saving a comrade. Counting coup was another tradition among some tribes, where a warrior gained honor by touching an enemy with a coup stick during battle without harming them, demonstrating extraordinary bravery and restraint. These acts of valor were celebrated within the community, reinforcing the warrior's role as a source of inspiration and pride.

Conflict among tribes was not uncommon, as groups competed for resources, hunting grounds, or territory. However, warfare among Native Americans was often different from the large-scale battles of European armies. It was typically characterized by small, strategic raids rather than prolonged campaigns. These raids required stealth, planning, and intimate knowledge of the terrain, skills at which Native American warriors excelled. Their ability to navigate their environment with precision gave them a significant advantage over less familiar enemies.

The arrival of European settlers brought new challenges and intensified the role of Native American Bravehearts. As settlers encroached on their lands, many tribes found themselves fighting to protect their homes and way of life. Leaders like Tecumseh of the Shawnee, Crazy Horse of the Lakota, and Geronimo of the Apache became legendary figures, known for their resistance against overwhelming odds. These leaders inspired their people to stand firm against the loss of their lands, culture, and independence.

Tecumseh, for instance, dreamed of uniting the tribes into a powerful confederation to resist the westward expansion of settlers. A brilliant strategist and orator, Tecumseh fought alongside his people in battles and worked tirelessly to forge alliances. His courage and vision made him a symbol of resistance and unity, even after his death in 1813. Crazy Horse, on the other hand, is remembered for his role in the Battle of the Little Bighorn, where he led his warriors to a stunning victory against the U.S. Army. His unwavering dedication to preserving his people's way of life made him a hero among the Lakota and an enduring figure in Native American history.

The story of Geronimo, the Apache leader, is another testament to the determination of Native American Bravehearts. For decades, Geronimo and his band of warriors resisted the encroachment of settlers and the U.S. government. Despite being outnumbered and outgunned, Geronimo's guerrilla tactics and knowledge of the harsh desert terrain allowed him to evade capture time and again. His defiance made him a symbol of resistance, and his eventual surrender in 1886 marked the end of an era of open Native American resistance.

For Native American Bravehearts, the fight was not only about physical survival but also about preserving their cultural identity. As European settlers brought new diseases, displaced tribes, and imposed foreign systems of government and religion, the role of the warrior evolved. Bravehearts became defenders of their traditions, keeping alive the stories, songs, and ceremonies that defined their people. They fought not only with weapons but also with words, actions, and the determination to pass on their heritage to future generations.

Today, the legacy of Native American Bravehearts lives on. Their courage, resilience, and deep connection to the land continue to inspire people around the world. Tribes honor their ancestors through ceremonies, powwows, and storytelling, keeping the spirit of the Bravehearts alive. Modern Native American leaders and activists draw on the strength of these warriors as they work to preserve their languages, lands, and rights. The image of the Braveheart, standing tall in the face of adversity, remains a powerful symbol of resistance, pride, and the enduring spirit of Native American culture.

# Chapter 17: The Siege Masters of Assyria

The Siege Masters of Assyria were among the most fearsome and innovative warriors of the ancient world. The Assyrian Empire, which dominated the Near East from roughly 900 BCE to 600 BCE, was renowned for its military might, and its success was built in large part on its mastery of siege warfare. These warriors and engineers transformed the art of war, developing techniques and technologies that enabled them to conquer some of the most heavily fortified cities of their time. Their reputation for ruthlessness and efficiency made them both feared and respected by their enemies, and their innovations laid the foundation for siege tactics used for centuries afterward.

At the height of their power, the Assyrians ruled over a vast empire that stretched from the Persian Gulf to the Mediterranean Sea, encompassing modern-day Iraq, Syria, Turkey, and parts of Iran and Egypt. This sprawling territory was secured through relentless military campaigns, and many of the cities and kingdoms they sought to conquer were protected by high walls, moats, and other fortifications. Rather than being deterred by these defenses, the Assyrians saw them as challenges to overcome, and they became experts at breaking through even the most formidable barriers.

The Assyrian army was a highly organized and disciplined force, with soldiers divided into specialized units. While infantry, cavalry, and chariotry played crucial roles in open battles, siege warfare required a different set of skills. The siege masters of Assyria were a combination of engineers, sappers, and elite warriors who worked together to dismantle the defenses of their enemies. Their work began long before the battle, as they gathered intelligence on the target city, studying its walls, gates, and terrain to develop a tailored strategy.

One of the key innovations of the Assyrians was their use of siege engines—massive, mobile machines designed to breach walls and gates. The battering ram was among their most iconic inventions. These large, wheeled structures housed a heavy wooden beam capped with a metal head, which soldiers would swing repeatedly against a wall or gate to weaken and eventually break through it. The battering ram was often protected by a wooden frame covered with wet hides to prevent it from catching fire, a common defensive tactic used by besieged cities.

Another formidable weapon in the Assyrian arsenal was the siege tower, a towering, mobile structure that allowed soldiers to scale walls while remaining protected from enemy fire. Siege towers were equipped with ladders, platforms, and sometimes even drawbridges that could be lowered onto the top of a wall. Archers stationed in the towers provided covering fire, picking off defenders and clearing the way for soldiers to storm the fortifications. These towers were feats of engineering, requiring significant resources and manpower to construct and maneuver.

In addition to these mechanical marvels, the Assyrians employed a range of other tactics to weaken and breach enemy defenses. Sappers, or specialized engineers, were tasked with undermining walls by digging tunnels beneath them. These tunnels were often propped up with wooden supports, which the sappers would set on fire once the excavation was complete. The resulting collapse would destabilize the wall above, creating a breach for the army to exploit. This technique required precision and courage, as sappers often worked under constant threat from enemy defenders.

The Assyrians were also masters of psychological warfare, using fear as a weapon to demoralize their enemies. They understood that the mere threat of a siege could sometimes be enough to force a city to surrender without a fight. Before launching an attack, the Assyrians would often send envoys to demand submission, warning of the dire consequences of resistance. These warnings were not idle threats; the Assyrians were notorious for their brutal treatment of conquered cities, which included massacres, enslavement, and public executions. Tales of their ruthlessness spread far and wide, and many cities chose to capitulate rather than face the wrath of the Assyrian army.

For those cities that did resist, the Assyrians were relentless. They would surround the city, cutting off supplies and starving the inhabitants into submission. This tactic, known as a siege blockade, could last for months or even years, depending on the strength of the city's defenses and its ability to withstand isolation. During this time, the Assyrians would continue their efforts to breach the walls, using their siege engines, sappers, and archers to apply constant pressure.

One of the most famous examples of Assyrian siege warfare is the conquest of Lachish, a fortified city in the Kingdom of Judah, around 701 BCE. This campaign is vividly depicted in a series of reliefs from the palace of King Sennacherib in Nineveh, which show the Assyrian army in action. The reliefs illustrate the use of battering rams, siege towers, and archers, as well as the grim aftermath of the battle, with captives being led away and executed. These images provide a rare and detailed glimpse into the tactics and technology of the Assyrian siege masters.

The success of the Assyrians in siege warfare was not only due to their advanced technology and tactics but also to their ability to adapt and innovate. They constantly refined their methods, learning from each campaign and incorporating new ideas. For example, they developed strategies to counter the use of fire by defenders, such as using metal sheathing on their siege engines and soaking wooden components in water. They also became experts at exploiting weaknesses in enemy fortifications, such as poorly defended gates or sections of wall built on unstable ground.

Despite their dominance, the Assyrians were not invincible. Their reliance on siege warfare required significant resources, and prolonged campaigns could strain their supply lines and manpower. As their empire grew larger, maintaining control over distant territories became increasingly difficult, and internal rebellions and external pressures eventually led to their downfall. By 612 BCE, the Assyrian capital of Nineveh was sacked by a coalition of enemies, marking the end of their empire.

The legacy of the Siege Masters of Assyria, however, endured long after the fall of their empire. Their innovations in siege technology and tactics influenced subsequent civilizations, including the Persians, Greeks, and Romans, who built upon and adapted Assyrian methods for their own conquests. The techniques developed by the Assyrians—such as the use of battering rams, siege towers, and sappers—remained staples of warfare for centuries, demonstrating the lasting impact of their military ingenuity.

The Assyrian siege masters were more than just warriors; they were engineers, strategists, and pioneers who transformed the art of war. Their ability to overcome seemingly insurmountable obstacles and their relentless pursuit of victory made them one of the most formidable forces of the ancient world. Their story is a testament to the power of innovation and determination, as well as a reminder of the complexities and consequences of war in human history.

# Chapter 18: Maori Warriors of New Zealand

Maori warriors of New Zealand were among the most skilled and formidable fighters in the Pacific, known for their bravery, discipline, and strong connection to their culture and land. The Maori people, the indigenous Polynesian inhabitants of New Zealand, have a proud warrior tradition deeply rooted in their customs, beliefs, and way of life. Their reputation as fierce fighters is matched by their commitment to honor, community, and spiritual connection. Through their distinctive weapons, tactics, and war dances, Maori warriors became symbols of strength and resilience.

The Maori worldview, or *te ao Māori*, shaped every aspect of their lives, including warfare. Central to this worldview was the concept of *mana*, a spiritual power or prestige that warriors sought to maintain or enhance through their actions. *Mana* was earned through success in battle, acts of leadership, and adherence to cultural principles. Conversely, losing a battle or acting dishonorably could diminish a warrior's *mana*. This spiritual aspect of war meant that fighting was not only about physical strength but also about upholding one's reputation, family, and tribe.

Warfare was an integral part of Maori society, often sparked by disputes over land, resources, or insults to honor. Tribal groups, or *iwi*, would go to battle to defend their territories, secure *utu* (a concept of balance or revenge), or gain prestige. Preparation for war was a communal effort, involving not only the warriors but also the wider tribe. Rituals and ceremonies played a significant role in ensuring the favor of the gods and the readiness of the warriors.

Training for Maori warriors began at a young age. Boys were taught the skills they would need to become effective fighters, including agility, endurance, and mastery of weapons. This training was both physical and mental, as warriors were expected to show courage and composure in the face of danger. They also learned the *haka*, a powerful war dance used to intimidate enemies and inspire their own forces. The *haka*, with its fierce facial expressions, stomping, and chanting, demonstrated the unity and determination of the warriors while channeling their collective energy.

Maori weapons were as distinctive as the warriors who wielded them, crafted from materials such as wood, bone, and greenstone (a type of jade). One of the most iconic weapons was the *taiaha*, a wooden staff with a pointed end for thrusting and a flat, blade-like end for striking. The *taiaha* required exceptional skill to use effectively, and its wielders were trained in a martial art called *mau rākau*, which emphasized precision, timing, and fluid movement. Another notable weapon was the *patu*, a short, club-like weapon often made of greenstone or whalebone. The *patu* was used for close combat, delivering swift and powerful blows.

The spiritual aspect of Maori warfare extended to their weapons, which were often imbued with symbolic meanings and passed down through generations. A warrior's weapon was considered an extension of their *mana*, and great care was taken in its creation and maintenance. Some weapons were adorned with intricate carvings that told stories of their lineage or depicted protective symbols. These carvings also reflected the artistry and craftsmanship of the Maori people.

Maori warfare was highly strategic, relying on a combination of discipline, teamwork, and intimate knowledge of the terrain. Warriors would often launch surprise attacks, using stealth and speed to overwhelm their enemies. They were also skilled in defensive tactics, constructing fortified villages called *pā*. These *pā* were strategically located on hills or ridges and featured palisades, trenches, and earthworks designed to repel invaders. The design of *pā* showcased the Maori's ingenuity and ability to adapt to their environment.

Before battle, Maori warriors performed rituals to prepare themselves spiritually and mentally. One of the most striking elements of this preparation was the *moko*, or facial tattoos, worn by many warriors.

The *moko* was not only a mark of status and identity but also a symbol of courage and endurance, as the tattooing process was extremely painful. Each *moko* was unique, telling the story of the warrior's lineage, achievements, and personality. The sight of tattooed faces and bodies on the battlefield was meant to intimidate enemies, reinforcing the warrior's fearsome reputation.

The *haka*, performed just before a battle, was another key element of Maori warfare. This dance was both a psychological weapon and a way to unite the warriors. Its powerful movements and chants expressed the warriors' readiness to fight and their defiance of the enemy. Watching a group of warriors perform the *haka* was a formidable sight, and even today, it remains a symbol of Maori pride and strength.

Despite their formidable skills, Maori warriors faced significant challenges with the arrival of European settlers in the late 18th and early 19th centuries. Europeans brought new weapons, such as muskets, which dramatically altered the nature of Maori warfare. The period known as the Musket Wars saw an arms race among Maori tribes, as those with access to firearms gained a significant advantage over those who relied on traditional weapons. This era was marked by widespread conflict, as tribes fought to expand their territories or settle old scores.

The introduction of European settlers also led to conflicts over land, culminating in the New Zealand Wars of the 19th century. Maori warriors played a central role in these wars, using their traditional skills and strategies alongside newly acquired firearms. They continued to construct *pā*, adapting their designs to counter the threat of artillery. The *pā* of this era were often temporary fortifications, built quickly and with great ingenuity to withstand sieges and bombardments.

Throughout these conflicts, Maori warriors demonstrated remarkable resilience and adaptability. Even when faced with the superior numbers and technology of British forces, they managed to achieve significant victories. Leaders such as Te Rauparaha, Hone Heke, and Te Kooti became legendary for their tactical brilliance and determination to defend their people and way of life.

Today, the legacy of Maori warriors is celebrated and honored as a vital part of New Zealand's cultural heritage. The skills, values, and traditions of these warriors are preserved through practices like *mau rākau* and the continued performance of the *haka*. Maori culture remains a vibrant and integral part of New Zealand's identity, and the stories of their brave ancestors inspire pride and respect among both Maori and non-Maori alike.

The Maori warrior spirit lives on not only in cultural practices but also in the contributions of Maori people to modern society. Many Maori serve with distinction in New Zealand's armed forces, carrying forward the traditions of courage, discipline, and honor that defined their ancestors. The enduring image of the Maori warrior, standing tall with weapon in hand and *mana* in heart, serves as a powerful reminder of the strength and resilience of the Maori people.

# Chapter 19: Heroes of Ancient India

The heroes of ancient India were legendary figures who displayed extraordinary courage, wisdom, and strength, becoming symbols of virtue and inspiration for generations. These warriors, kings, and sages were not only skilled in battle but also deeply rooted in spiritual and moral principles, often guided by a strong sense of duty or *dharma*. Their stories are preserved in epics, historical texts, and oral traditions, painting a rich tapestry of heroism and legacy.

One of the most celebrated heroes of ancient India is Arjuna, the great warrior prince from the *Mahabharata*, one of the longest and most intricate epics in the world. Arjuna was renowned for his unparalleled skill with the bow and arrow, earning the title of the greatest archer of his time. He was a member of the Pandavas, five brothers who were central to the epic's grand tale of righteousness and familial conflict. Arjuna's heroism was defined not only by his abilities as a warrior but also by his unwavering devotion to *dharma*. His most famous moment came during the great Kurukshetra War, when he hesitated to fight against his own family members and sought guidance from his charioteer, Lord Krishna. The advice he received became the foundation of the *Bhagavad Gita*, a sacred text that addresses the complexities of duty, morality, and the nature of existence.

Another legendary figure is Rama, the virtuous king from the epic *Ramayana*. Rama is celebrated as the epitome of honor, loyalty, and righteousness. Born as the prince of Ayodhya, he was exiled to the forest for fourteen years due to palace intrigue. During this exile, his wife Sita was abducted by the demon king Ravana, leading Rama to embark on an epic quest to rescue her. With the help of Hanuman, the monkey god, and an army of devoted allies, Rama waged a fierce battle against Ravana, showcasing his courage and determination. Rama's story is not only about his heroism in battle but also about his adherence to *dharma* even in the face of immense personal sacrifice. He is revered as an ideal king, husband, and leader, embodying values that remain deeply ingrained in Indian culture.

Hanuman, one of Rama's closest allies, is another iconic hero of ancient India. Known for his immense strength, loyalty, and devotion, Hanuman played a pivotal role in the *Ramayana*. His feats include leaping across the ocean to locate Sita in Ravana's kingdom and setting the city of Lanka ablaze with his fiery tail. Despite his extraordinary powers, Hanuman is also celebrated for his humility and unwavering dedication to Rama. He represents the ideals of selfless service and devotion, inspiring countless followers who honor him as a divine protector.

Moving beyond mythology, ancient India was also home to real-life warrior kings who displayed remarkable bravery and leadership. Chandragupta Maurya, the founder of the Mauryan Empire, was one such hero. Rising from humble beginnings, Chandragupta, with the guidance of his mentor Chanakya, united much of the Indian subcontinent under one rule. His empire became one of the largest and most powerful in the ancient world, known for its administrative efficiency and military strength. Chandragupta's legacy is a testament to the power of determination and strategic vision.

Ashoka the Great, Chandragupta's grandson, is another monumental figure in ancient Indian history. Initially known for his military conquests, Ashoka's transformation from a ruthless warrior to a proponent of peace and Buddhism is one of the most remarkable stories of ancient times. After witnessing the immense suffering caused by his conquests, particularly during the Kalinga War, Ashoka embraced Buddhism and dedicated his life to spreading its teachings. He built stupas, inscribed edicts promoting non-violence and tolerance, and worked to improve the welfare of his people. Ashoka's journey from a conqueror to a compassionate ruler makes him a unique hero, embodying the ideals of forgiveness, wisdom, and humility.

Other notable heroes include the Rajput warriors, who emerged during the later periods of ancient India but carried forward the heroic traditions of their predecessors. Rajput leaders like Prithviraj Chauhan are celebrated for their valor and resistance against foreign invasions. Known for their code of honor and chivalry, Rajputs exemplified the warrior ethos, often choosing death over dishonor in battle.

Ancient Indian heroines also played significant roles in shaping the narratives of heroism. Sita, from the *Ramayana*, is admired not only for her beauty and grace but also for her steadfastness and moral strength during her abduction and captivity. Draupadi, the queen of the Pandavas in the *Mahabharata*, is another powerful figure. Her intelligence, resilience, and dignity, even in the face of humiliation, make her one of the most respected women in Indian mythology.

Indian heroes were not only warriors but also sages and scholars who wielded the power of knowledge. Rishi Vishwamitra, who was once a king, became one of the most revered sages through his dedication to spiritual pursuits. His transformation from a warrior to a sage exemplifies the idea that heroism is not limited to the battlefield but can also be found in the quest for wisdom and self-mastery. Similarly, figures like Chanakya, the brilliant strategist and political thinker, used their intellect to guide rulers and shape the destiny of the nation.

Ancient Indian culture also emphasized the importance of heroes as protectors of their communities and upholders of justice. This is evident in the tales of Krishna, a multifaceted hero who played a key role in the *Mahabharata* and is also worshipped as a deity. Krishna's life is filled with heroic deeds, from his childhood adventures defeating demons to his guidance of Arjuna on the battlefield. He is celebrated for his courage, wisdom, and playful spirit, embodying the idea that heroism can be both profound and joyful.

The legacy of ancient Indian heroes continues to resonate in modern times. Their stories are passed down through generations in the form of epics, folklore, and festivals, keeping their spirit alive. These heroes are not just remembered for their physical strength or victories but also for their adherence to values like compassion, humility, and duty. They inspire people to strive for greatness while remaining rooted in principles that uplift society.

From the mythical heroes of the *Mahabharata* and *Ramayana* to the historical figures who shaped the course of Indian history, the heroes of ancient India embody a rich tradition of courage, wisdom, and moral integrity. Their stories remind us that true heroism lies not just in defeating enemies but in upholding values that bring harmony and justice to the world. Their enduring legacy serves as a source of inspiration, teaching us that the qualities of a hero—strength, resilience, and a commitment to doing what is right—are timeless and universal.

# Chapter 20: The Code of the Ninja Shadows

The Code of the Ninja Shadows is a mysterious and fascinating part of history, shrouded in secrecy and intrigue. Ninjas, also known as *shinobi*, were covert agents of feudal Japan, and their code of conduct was deeply rooted in discipline, strategy, and adaptability. Unlike the warriors who fought on open battlefields, ninjas operated in the shadows, relying on stealth, intelligence, and cunning to achieve their goals. Their way of life was governed by unwritten rules that emphasized survival, loyalty, and the mastery of their craft, making them one of the most enigmatic and skilled groups of warriors in history.

Ninjas were not bound by a single, formalized code like the samurai, who followed *bushido*, the "way of the warrior." Instead, their code was practical and flexible, adapting to the demands of espionage and unconventional warfare. At the heart of their ethos was the principle of secrecy. A ninja's identity, mission, and methods were closely guarded, often hidden even from their own families. This veil of mystery allowed them to blend into society, moving unnoticed among commoners and elites alike. Their ability to become "invisible" was one of their greatest strengths, and it set them apart from other warriors of their time.

Training to become a ninja began at a young age and was incredibly rigorous. Aspiring ninjas, often drawn from the lower classes, were taught to harness their environment, turning ordinary objects into tools of survival and warfare. They learned to climb walls, leap across rooftops, and navigate treacherous terrains with ease. The training also included mastering the art of disguise, allowing ninjas to assume different identities, such as merchants, monks, or farmers. By blending into their surroundings, they could gather intelligence or strike when least expected.

Stealth was the cornerstone of the ninja's skill set. They perfected silent movement, walking in such a way that their footsteps made no sound. They used special footwear called *tabi*, split-toed socks, and lightweight shoes that helped them move quietly. Ninjas were also experts at hiding in plain sight, using shadows, natural features, and even psychological tricks to avoid detection. This ability to disappear at a moment's notice became legendary, earning them a reputation as almost supernatural beings.

Another key aspect of the ninja code was resourcefulness. Ninjas were trained to use whatever was at hand to complete their missions. Their tools and weapons were often simple yet highly effective. The *kunai*, a small, multi-purpose blade, could be used as a weapon, climbing tool, or digging implement. The *shuriken*, or throwing star, was not only a weapon but also a distraction device. They even used smoke bombs to create confusion and escape. Ninjas often carried items like grappling hooks, caltrops (spiked devices to slow pursuers), and collapsible ladders, showcasing their creativity and ingenuity.

The ninjas' arsenal also included knowledge of nature and survival. They understood how to navigate by the stars, use plants for medicine or poison, and predict weather patterns. This deep connection to their environment allowed them to remain self-sufficient and operate in remote or hostile areas. Their adaptability extended to their combat skills, which focused on efficiency rather than honor. Ninjas trained in a martial art called *ninjutsu*, which emphasized practical techniques for self-defense, offense, and escape. Unlike samurai, who valued direct confrontations, ninjas were taught to avoid unnecessary battles and prioritize the success of their mission.

Loyalty to their clan was another pillar of the ninja code. Ninjas often worked in small, close-knit groups or served powerful warlords, known as *daimyo*, who hired them for espionage, sabotage, or assassination. A ninja's loyalty to their employer was paramount, but they also maintained a strong sense of camaraderie within their own ranks.

Their missions required absolute trust and coordination, as even the smallest mistake could mean failure or death.

Despite their reputation as assassins, ninjas were not mindless killers. They valued strategy and intelligence over brute force, often using psychological warfare to outwit their enemies. For example, they might spread rumors to demoralize an opposing army or plant fake documents to mislead their targets. Their ability to manipulate information made them highly effective spies, and their activities often had a significant impact on the political and military landscape of feudal Japan.

The spiritual aspect of the ninja code cannot be overlooked. Many ninjas practiced meditation and other disciplines to sharpen their minds and maintain focus. They sought to achieve a state of *zen*, where their actions became instinctive and free of hesitation. This mental clarity was crucial for their dangerous missions, where split-second decisions could mean the difference between success and failure. Ninjas also believed in the power of *ki*, or life energy, and trained to harness it for physical and mental strength.

One of the most enduring aspects of the ninja legacy is their role as protectors and avengers. While their methods were unconventional, ninjas often fought for causes they believed were just, such as defending their homeland or supporting oppressed communities. In some stories, they are portrayed as heroic figures who stood against tyranny and corruption, using their skills to level the playing field against more powerful foes.

The golden age of ninjas was during Japan's Sengoku period (1467–1615), a time of constant warfare and political intrigue. During this era, their skills were in high demand, and they became indispensable to warlords vying for power. The Iga and Koga clans, in particular, were renowned for their expertise in ninjutsu. These clans operated from remote mountain regions, where they honed their skills and passed down their knowledge through generations.

As Japan entered a period of unification under the Tokugawa shogunate, the need for ninjas declined. The strict control imposed by the shogunate reduced the opportunities for covert operations, and the ninja way of life gradually faded into obscurity. However, their legacy lived on through stories, folklore, and popular culture, where they were immortalized as shadowy warriors of unparalleled skill.

Today, the ninja code continues to capture the imagination of people around the world. Their blend of discipline, ingenuity, and mystique serves as a reminder of the power of adaptability and resourcefulness. Modern martial artists and enthusiasts study *ninjutsu* not only to learn combat techniques but also to embrace the mental and spiritual principles that made the ninjas so remarkable.

The Code of the Ninja Shadows is more than just a guide to survival and combat; it is a testament to the human spirit's ability to overcome challenges through creativity, resilience, and determination. Whether as spies, warriors, or symbols of mystery, the ninjas of ancient Japan remain one of history's most intriguing and enduring legends. Their legacy teaches us that true strength lies not only in physical prowess but also in the mind and heart.

# Epilogue

The warriors of the ancient world may have long since left the battlefield, but their stories continue to inspire us. Through their courage, discipline, and sense of honor, they remind us of what it means to stand up for what you believe in, to protect those you care about, and to persevere in the face of great challenges.

Though centuries have passed, the values that guided these warriors—bravery, loyalty, and resilience—are as important today as they were in ancient times. Their stories are more than tales of combat; they are lessons in determination and leadership, proof that even in the most difficult moments, individuals have the power to shape history.

As we look back on their lives, we also see how their actions helped build civilizations, defend cultures, and inspire legends that still captivate our imaginations. From the mighty Spartan phalanxes to the silent steps of the ninja, each warrior brought something unique to the tapestry of human history.

The weapons they wielded may now rest in museums, and the battlefields they once fought on may be quiet, but their legacy lives on. Every time we hear their stories, we honor the courage and sacrifices that defined them.

As you close this book, take a moment to reflect on the warriors' unwavering commitment to their ideals. Let their courage inspire you to face your own challenges with determination and strength. The ancient world may be behind us, but the spirit of its warriors will always endure.

The End.

Milton Keynes UK
Ingram Content Group UK Ltd.
UKHW031046291124
451807UK00001B/85

9 798230 883142